Alfred's Premier Piano Course

Dennis Alexander • Gayle Kowalchyk • E. L. Lancaster • Victoria McArthur • Martha Mier

Alfred's *Premier Piano Course* Christmas Book 1A includes familiar Christmas pieces that reinforce concepts included in Lesson Book 1A. The music continues the strong pedagogical focus of the course while providing the enjoyment of playing familiar music during the Christmas season. Duet accompaniments create rich sounds and can aid the student with rhythmic security. Both solo and duet parts contain measure numbers for easy reference.

Christmas Book 1A is not correlated page-by-page with Lesson Book 1A. However, the pieces use only the concepts that are introduced in Lesson Book 1A and can be studied after the student has begun reading on the staff (pages 32–64). They are arranged in progressive order of difficulty with the easiest pieces first, though it is not necessary to progress straight through the book. Christmas 1A also can be used to supplement any beginning piano method.

Allowing students to study music they enjoy during the Christmas season is highly motivating. Consequently, reading and rhythm skills often improve greatly when studying holiday music. The authors hope that the music in Christmas 1A brings hours of enjoyment to this festive season. Merry Christmas!

Edited by Morton Manus

Cover Design by Ted Engelbart
Interior Design by Tom Gerou
Illustrations by Jimmy Holder
Music Engraving by Linda Lusk

Copyright © MMVIII by Alfred Publishing Co., Inc.
All Rights Reserved.   Printed in USA.
ISBN-10: 0-7390-5491-0
ISBN-13: 978-0-7390-5491-8

CONTENTS

Good King Wenceslas

Good King Wenceslas tells the story of a Duke of Bohemia who always visited poor people on Christmas day. Even in the worst weather, he knocked on doors with gifts of food, clothing and firewood. John Mason Neale, an Englishman, wrote the lyrics in 1853 to fit a melody whose original words were about Spring.

Moderately fast

Traditional
Words by John Mason Neale

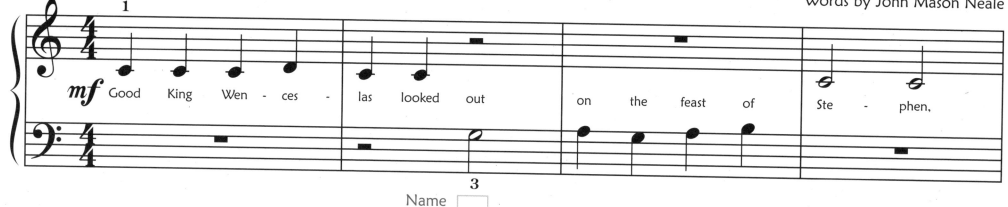

mf Good King Wen - ces - las looked out on the feast of Ste - phen,

Name note.

Duet: Student plays one octave higher.

Moderately fast

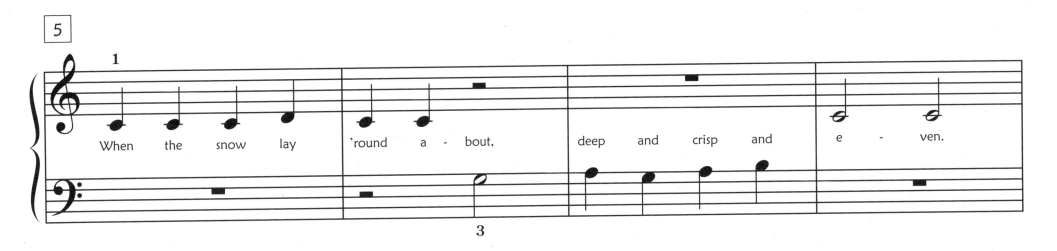

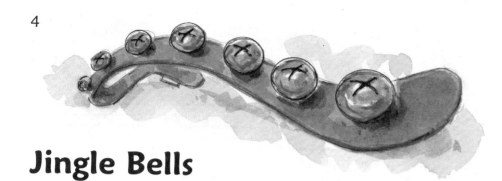

Jingle Bells

Both the words and music of **Jingle Bells** were written by James S. Pierpont of Boston in 1857. It was intended for Sunday School children to sing on a Thanksgiving program. The church members liked the piece so much that it was repeated on the Christmas program a few weeks later. Originally titled One Horse Open Sleigh, it soon became known as Jingle Bells since those words are used so often in the song.

James S. Pierpont

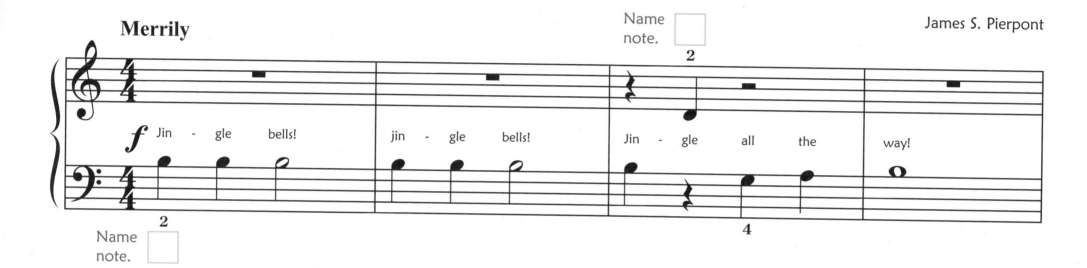

Duet: Student plays one octave higher.

5

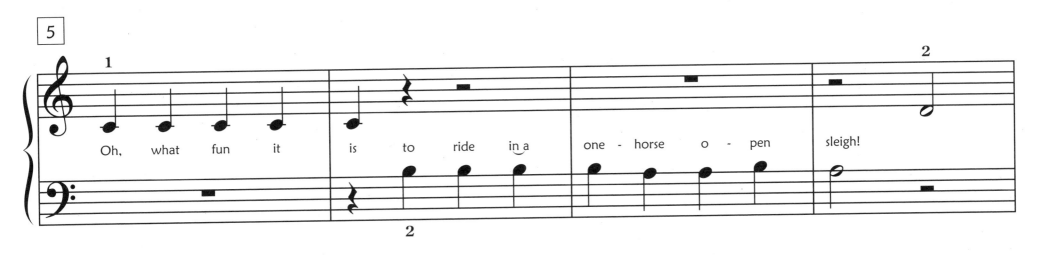

Jolly Old Saint Nicholas

Jolly Old Saint Nicholas is about a conversation between a young child and Santa Claus about the gifts that Santa might bring for Christmas. Nothing is known about the composer of the music or the author of the words. Most likely, it was written sometime in the late 19th century or the early 20th century.

Happily

Name note. ☐

Traditional

mf Jol - ly old Saint | Nich - o - las, | lean your ear this | way!

Duet: Student plays one octave higher.

Happily

5

Don't you tell a sin - gle soul what I'm going to say;

Name note. **2**

9

p Christ - mas Eve is com - ing soon, now, you dear old man;

13

whis - per what you'll bring to me, ***mf*** tell me if you can!

2

8

Up on the Housetop

Benjamin R. Hanby, a minister from Ohio, wrote the words and music for **Up on the Housetop** around 1860. Some think that it was inspired by Clement Clarke Moore's poem "A Visit from St. Nicholas." The words announce the arrival of Santa's sleigh on the roof and his journey down the chimney with toys for the children.

Quickly

Benjamin R. Hanby

Name note. ☐

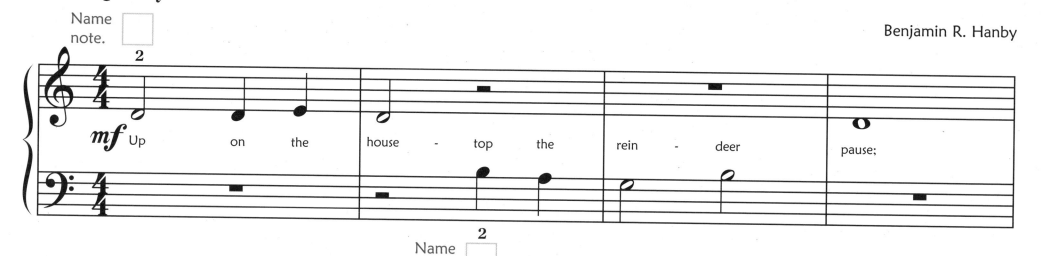

Up on the house - top the rein - deer pause;

Name note. ☐

Duet: Student plays one octave higher.

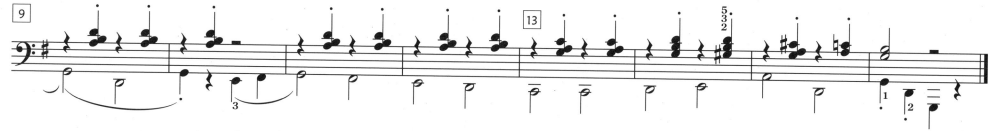

5

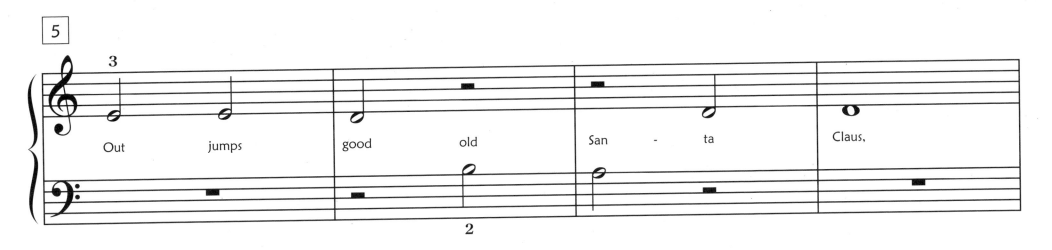

Out   jumps   good   old   San - ta   Claus,

9

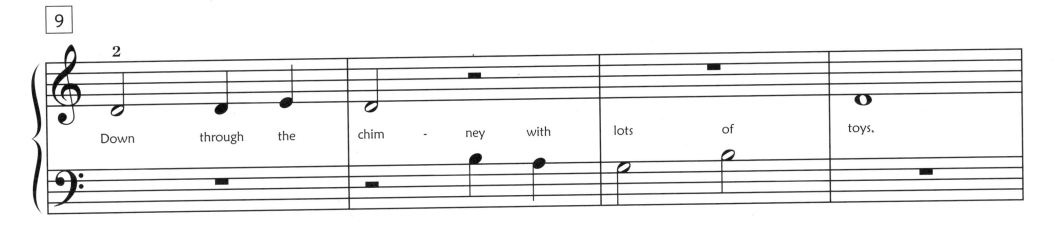

Down   through   the   chim - ney   with   lots   of   toys,

13

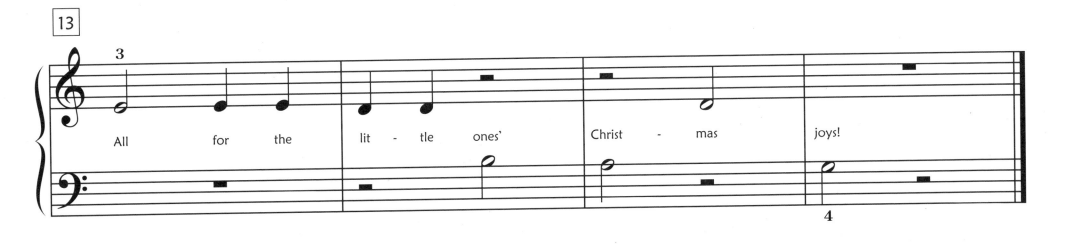

All   for   the   lit - tle   ones'   Christ - mas   joys!

Away in a Manger

The lullaby **Away in a Manger** was written by James R. Murray of Pennsylvania around 1885. Murray worked as a music editor and hymn writer throughout his life. When it was first published, Murray suggested that the words were written by Martin Luther, and entitled it Luther's Cradle Hymn. Researchers now know that this is not true, but the myth about the piece still exists.

Slowly

Name note.

James R. Murray

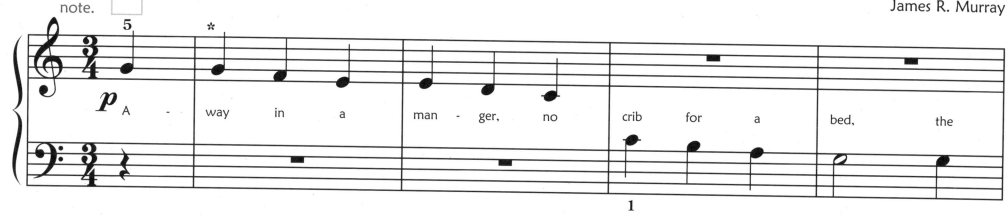

A - way in a man - ger, no crib for a bed, the

Duet: Student plays one octave higher.

Slowly

* Note to Teacher: In measures 1, 5, 9 and 13, students may substitute the following rhythm: ♩. ♫

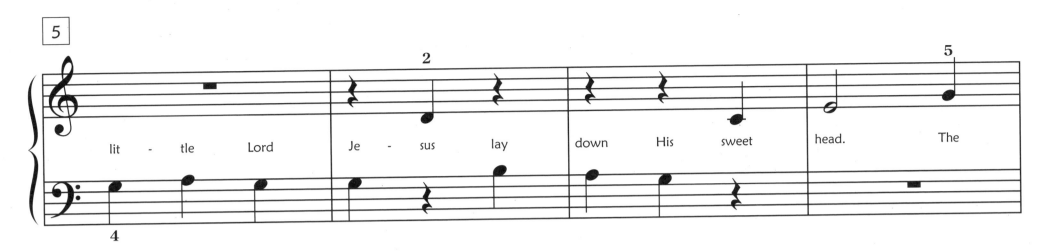

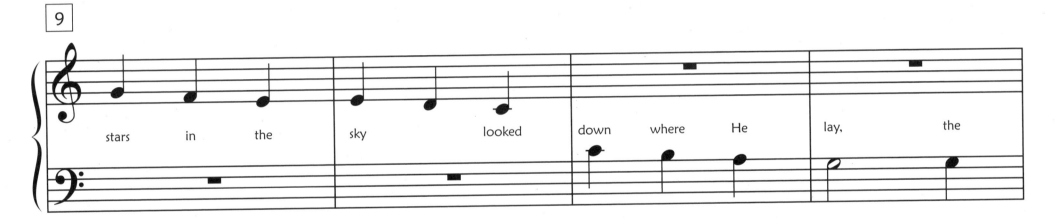

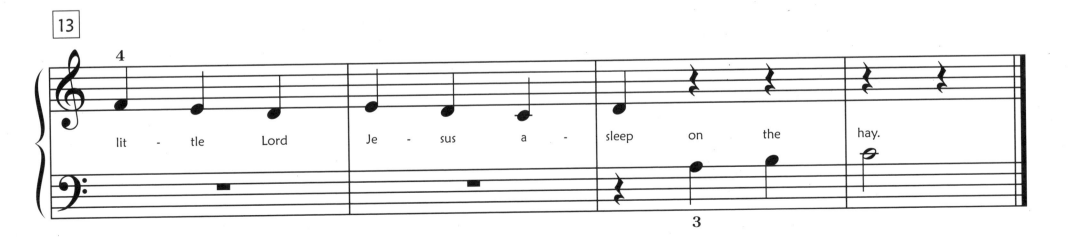

Go, Tell It on the Mountain

The lively spiritual **Go, Tell It on the Mountain** tells the story of the shepherds when they heard about the birth of the Baby Jesus. The song was made popular by performances of the Fisk University Jubilee Singers of Nashville. Some think that the music was written by Frederick Jerome Work and the words were by his brother John Wesley Work, a professor at Fisk University.

Brightly

Name note. ☐ 3

Traditional

Duet: Student plays one octave higher.

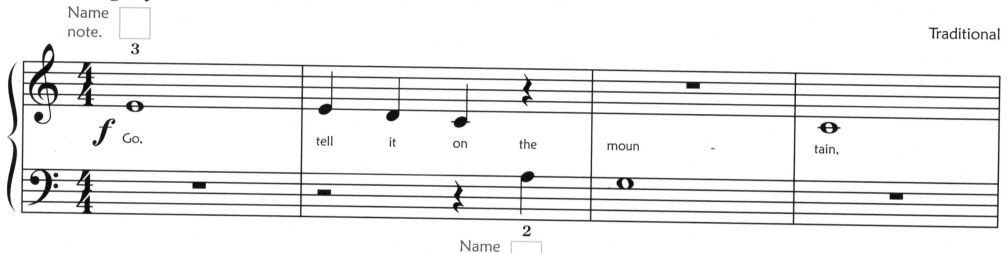

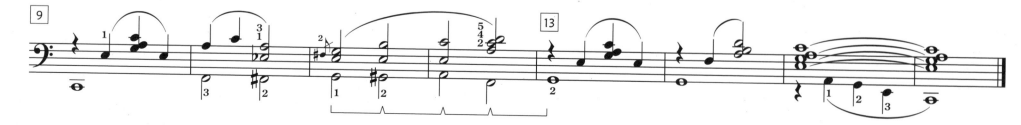

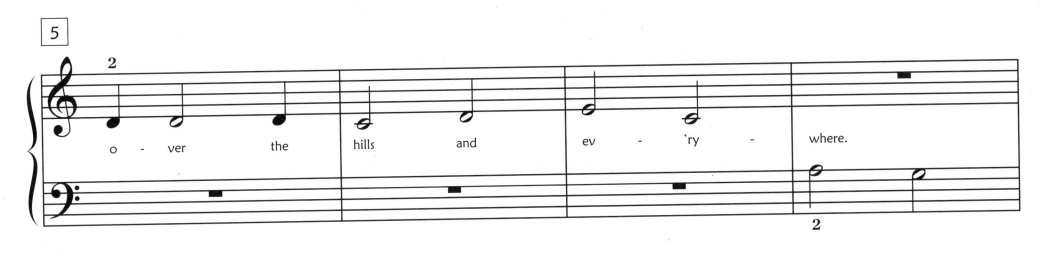

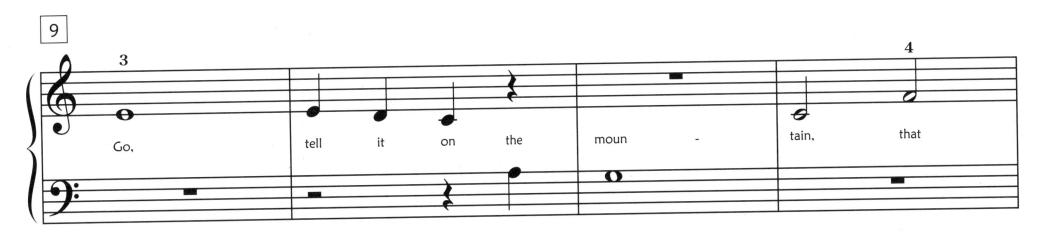

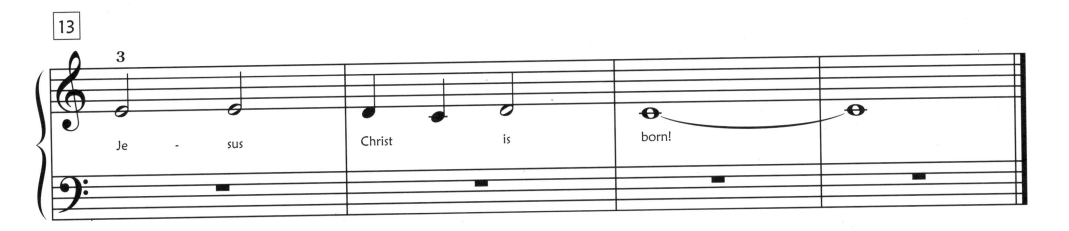

We Three Kings of Orient Are

We Three Kings of Orient Are is about the story of the Three Kings and their visit to bring gifts of gold, frankincense and myrrh to the Baby Jesus. The kings arrived on the twelfth night after the birth of Jesus, and the tradition of giving gifts on the twelfth night after Christmas still continues in some countries. The words and the music were written in 1857 by John Henry Hopkins, Jr. from Pennsylvania.

Moderately

John Henry Hopkins, Jr.

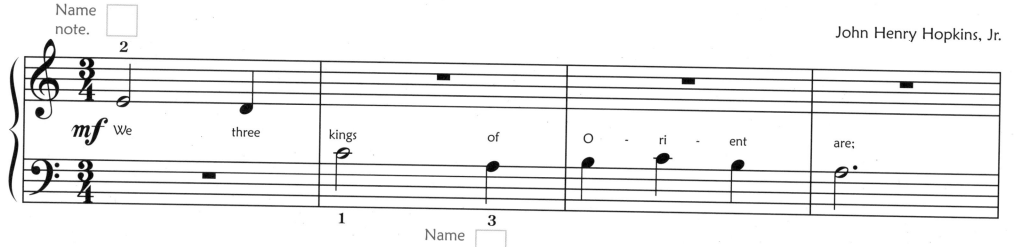

Duet: Student plays one octave higher.

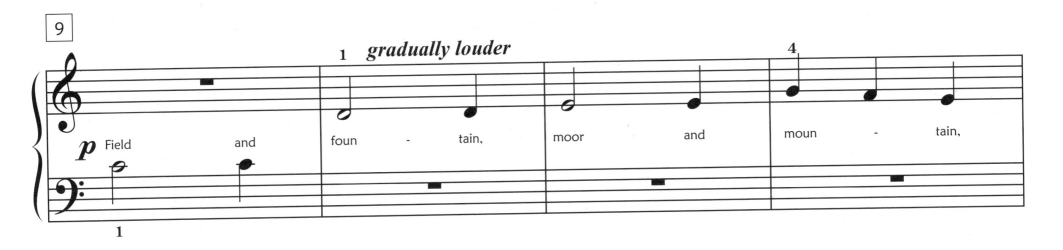

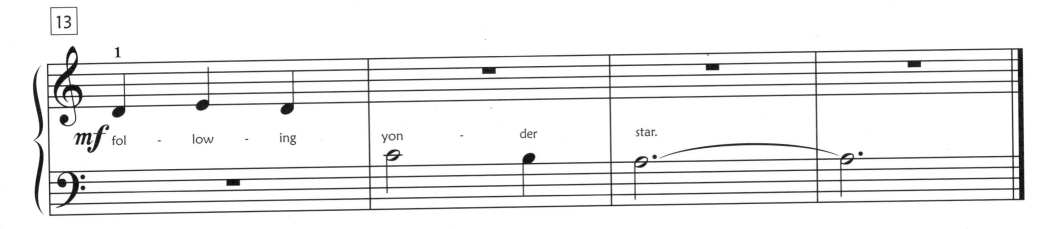

O Come, Little Children

O Come, Little Children, a German carol, was written by Johann Schulz with words by Christoph von Schmid in the late 1700s. The words invite children to visit the manger to see the humble place where the Baby Jesus was born.

Moderately

Name note.

Words by Christoph von Schmid
Music by Johann Schulz

O come, lit - tle chil - dren, come one and come all. O

Name note.

Duet: Student plays one octave higher.

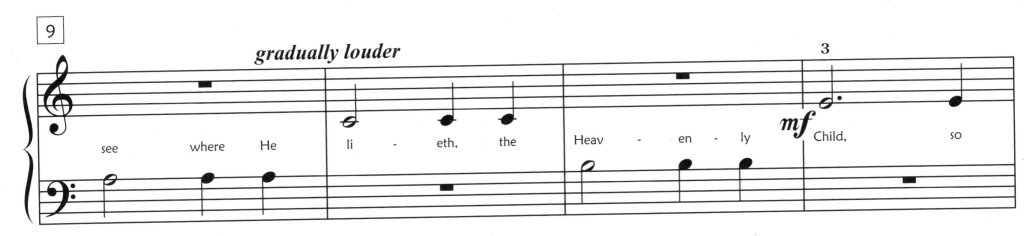

O Come, All Ye Faithful

O Come, All Ye Faithful was probably written around 1751 by the Englishman John Francis Wade who lived in France. Wade earned his living from copying and selling music as well as teaching music lessons. He originally wrote the words in Latin and they were translated into English in 1841 by an English minister, Frederick Oakeley.

John Francis Wade

Name note.

Duet: Student plays one octave higher.

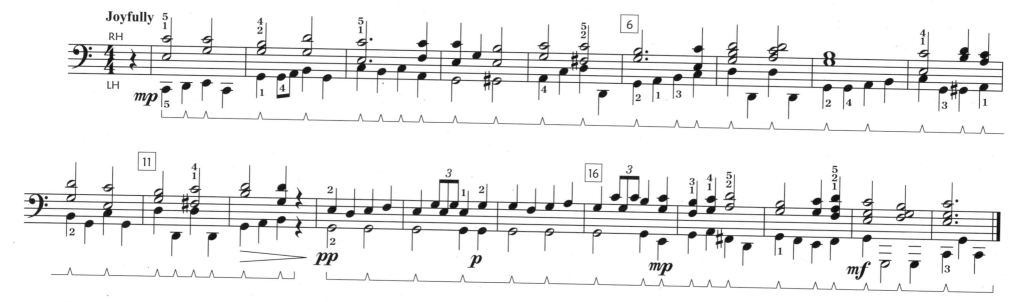

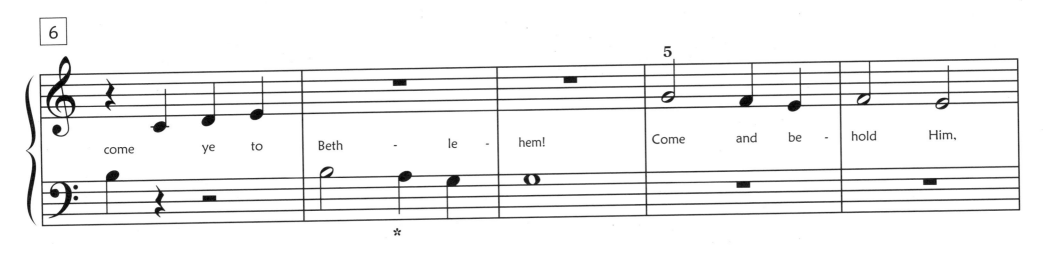

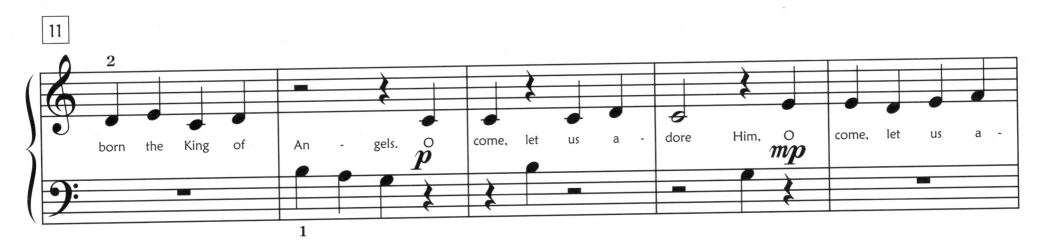

* **Note to Teacher:** In measures 7, 19 (beats 3 and 4) and 12 (beats 1 and 2), students may substitute the following rhythm: ♩. ♪

Dance of the Reed Flutes
(from *The Nutcracker*)

Dance of the Reed Flutes *is from Tchaikovsky's popular ballet, The Nutcracker. In the ballet the two main characters, Clara and the Prince, visit the Kingdom of Sweets and meet the beautiful Sugarplum Fairy. The couple enjoys several dances performed by those who live in the Kingdom of Sweets. Dance of the Reed Flutes is one of these popular dances.*

Moderately fast

Peter Ilyich Tchaikovsky

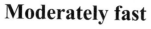

Name note.

Duet: Student plays **two** octaves higher.

Moderately fast

* Play the quarter notes short and detached.

O Come,
O Come Emmanuel

> **O Come, O Come Emmanuel** is one of the oldest Christmas carols. It was probably written by a monk as early as 800 A.D. The original version was written in Latin and was translated into English by John Mason Neale in 1851. The popular chorus, beginning with the words "Rejoice! Rejoice!," was added later.

Tenderly

Name note.

Traditional

mf O come, O come Em - man - u - el, and ran - som cap - tive

Name note.

Duet: Student plays one octave higher.

23

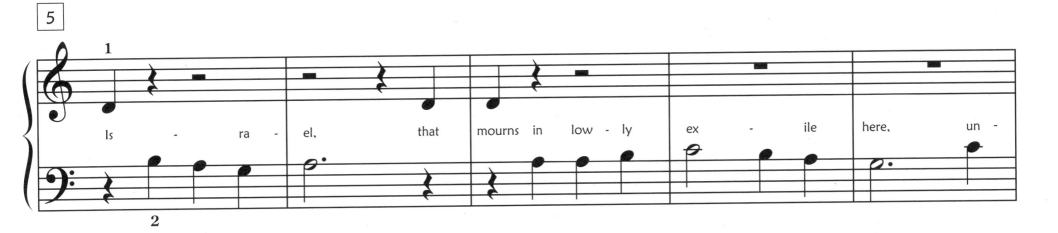

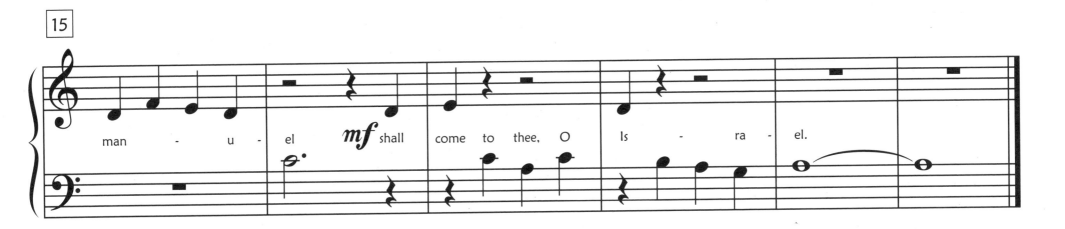